MULTICULTURAL CLIP-ART

**Designed & Illustrated By
Darcy Myers**

Publishers
T.S. Denison and Company, Inc.
Minneapolis, Minnesota 55431

T.S. DENISON

DEDICATION

To my Mother, Father, and to my grandparents,
who read to me as a child—
and to all those who read aloud to children,
helping them find the wonder of far-off places
through the magic of books.

Standard Book Number: 513-02179-5
Multicultural Clip-Art
Copyright by T.S. Denison & Company, Inc.
9601 Newton Avenue South
Minneapolis, Minnesota 55431

TABLE OF CONTENTS

Introduction

Multicultural Clip-Art is a tremendous resource that can be used to accompany a wide variety of thematic social studies units. The art is designed around twenty different countries and continents. Teachers are spending more time in the classroom introducing children to exciting new places and cultures from around the world. *Multicultural Clip-Art* is designed to reinforce and enhance the teaching of these instructional units.

For each country/continent, the national flag; traditional costume; animals; architecture; special events; and traditions have been illustrated. The illustrations can be enlarged or reduced on a photocopy machine or opaque projector.

These beautiful illustrations can made into colorful and creative bulletin boards and wall displays, puppets for oral language development, stationery for creative writing or home-school communication, art projects to accompany specific social studies topics, and teacher-created activity sheets. *Multicultural Clip-Art* is a resource that all teachers and students will learn from and enjoy using.

The flag of Nigeria—
Africa's most
populated country.

AFRICA

AFRICA

Giraffes like to feed on the savannas; their long necks help them reach the top branches of the thorn trees.

Bottle-shaped baobab trees in Madagascar store water in their spongy trunks.

Lions are among the many wild cats that live in Africa.

AFRICA

Houses are built on wooden stilts in the coastal village of Ganvie, Benin. Saltwater lagoons serve as streets and people travel on them with canoes.

A fisherman poles his reed boat across the calm surface of Lake Chad.

African dancer of
Zimbabwe

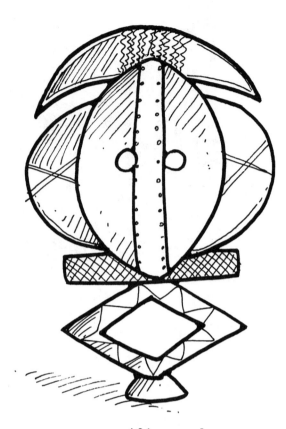

African mask

A *nauga* (harp) is
made from a skin
stretched over a log.

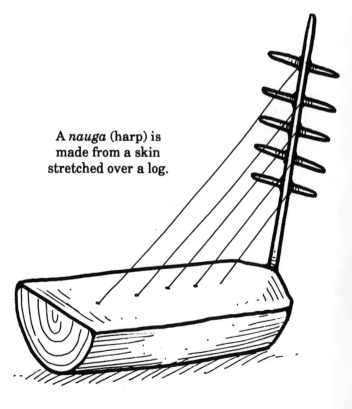

AUSTRALIA

The echidna, or spiny anteater, is one of only two mammals that lays eggs—the platypus is the other.

A long, strong tail helps the kangaroo balance.

A koala rides on its mother's back for 4–5 months after it has left the pouch.

platypus

The wombat digs burrows underground to escape from the heat.

A Tiwi (aborigine) boy carries a basket woven from strips of bark.

Surfing is a favorite Australian sport.

BRAZIL

BRAZIL

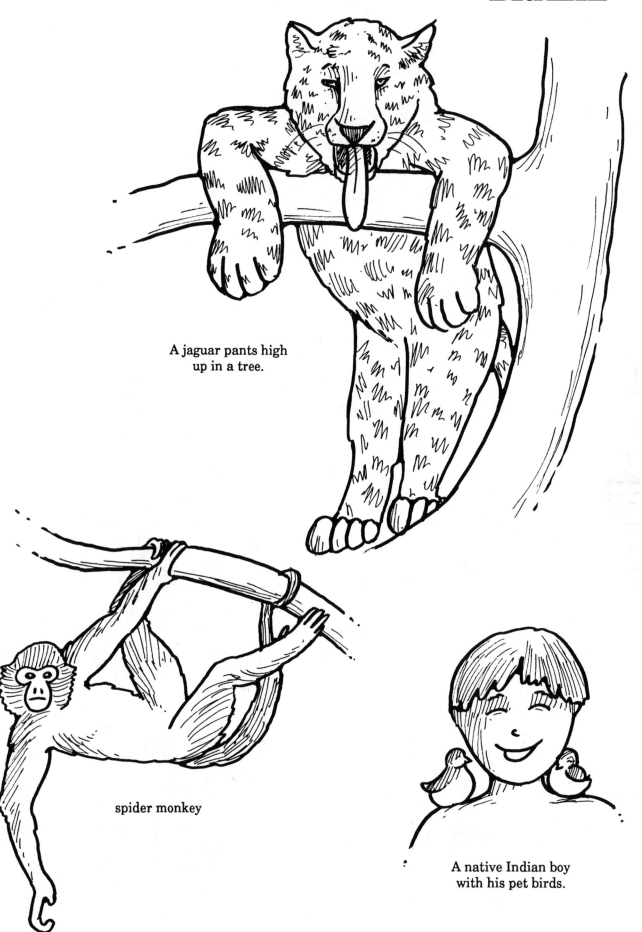

A jaguar pants high
up in a tree.

spider monkey

A native Indian boy
with his pet birds.

BRAZIL

The Opera House in Manaus was built in 1910 with money from the rubber industry.

Samba dancers dress
in elaborate costume
for the carnival.

Copacabana Beach in
Rio de Janeiro

CANADA

red maple leaf
(symbol of Canada)

snow goose

moose

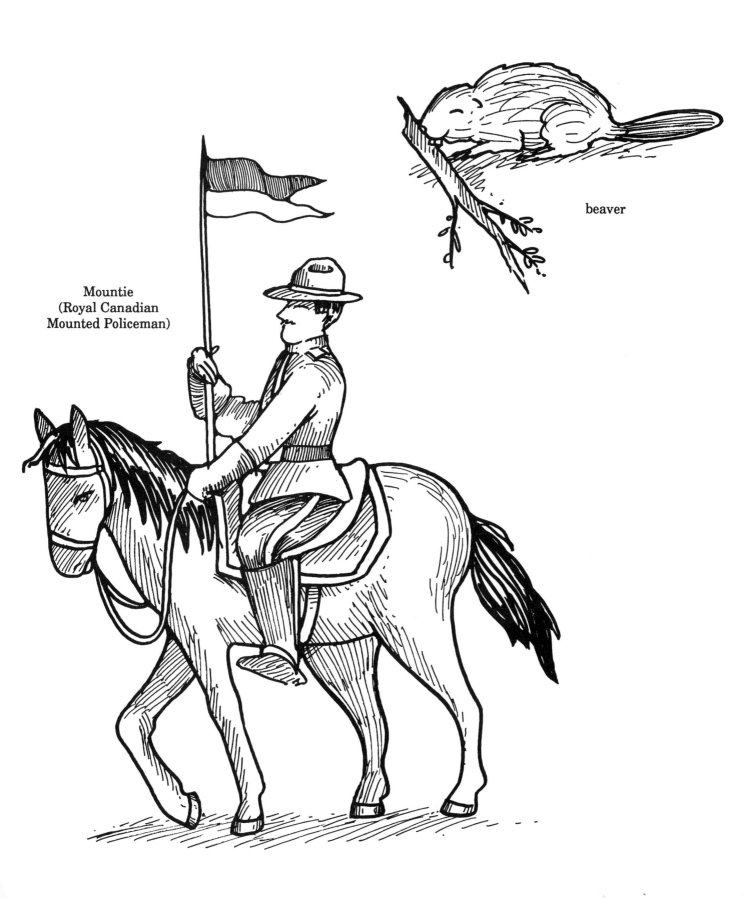

beaver

Mountie
(Royal Canadian
Mounted Policeman)

Totem pole of the
Northwest Pacific
Coast Indians.

hockey player

husky with sled

CHINA

giant panda

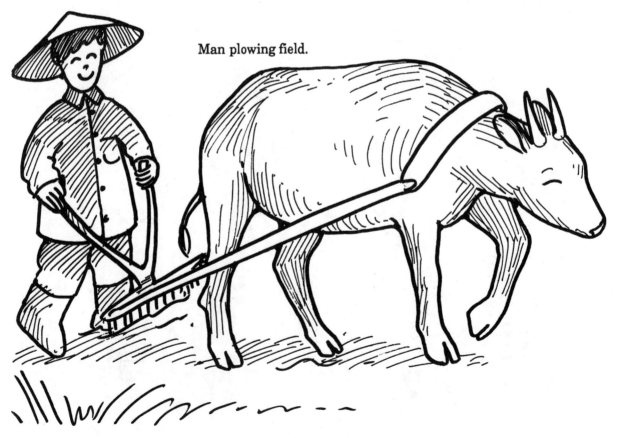

Man plowing field.

CHINA

The Great Wall

The Hall of Prayer for
Good Harvests,
Temple of Heaven

Schoolgirl playing
the P'i P'a.

dragon at
Chinese New Year

A man and his son
on a bicycle.

Both young and old
enjoy Tai Chi.

ENGLAND

ENGLAND

The European hare in its "boxing" position.

A mute swan swims in a pond in southwestern England

The Tower of London, an eleventh century fortress.

Stonehenge

Big Ben

English actors have
performed the
plays of
William Shakespeare
for many centuries.

guard at
Buckingham Palace

Some of the
"crown" jewels.

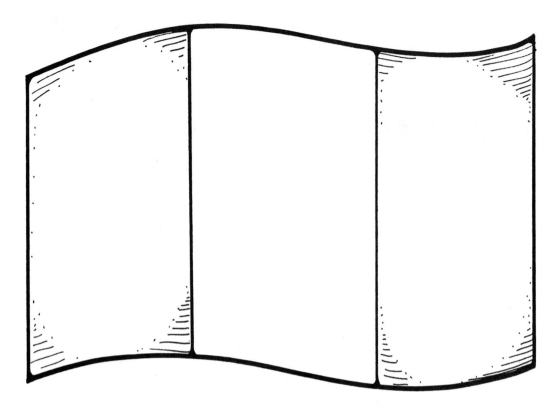

FRANCE

FRANCE

Geese are a common sight on country farms.

A sprig of lily is often worn in the button-hole as a May Day decoration.

French wine, French bread or "baguettes," fresh fruit, and a variety of cheeses make a perfect light meal!

FRANCE

Eiffel Tower

Notre Dame
Cathedral

A bicyclist racing
in the famous
Tour de France.

A man feeds the
birds in Paris.

A young girl marches
in an annual
Bastille Day Parade.

GERMANY

GERMANY

Wild boar still roam
in the larger forests
of Germany.

GERMANY

The Brandenburg Gate stands on the line that once divided East and West Berlin.

Neuschwanstein Castle

Musicians perform at
Munich's famous
"Oktoberfest."

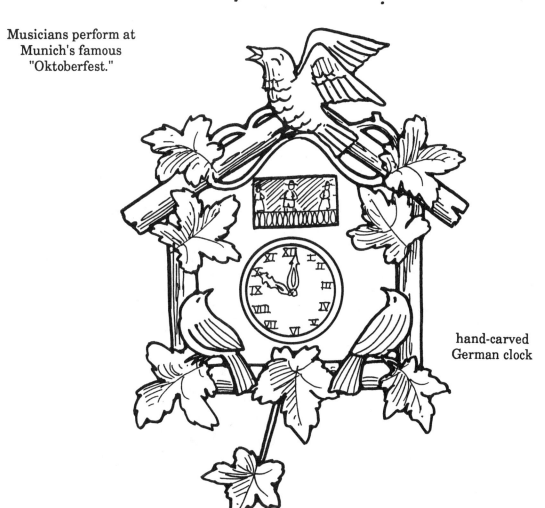

hand-carved
German clock

GREECE

GREECE

Gnarled olive trees in groves are a familiar sight in Greece.

Grapes are pressed twice to make wine— first by human feet and then by a screw-press.

The Parthenon was built in 447 B.C. and is a perfect example of classical architecture.

This church of Sifnos is snowy white—typical of many island buildings.

GREECE

A fisherman mends his net—using his feet as well as his hands.

A woman spins thread by hand...a method much older than wheel-spinning.

INDIA

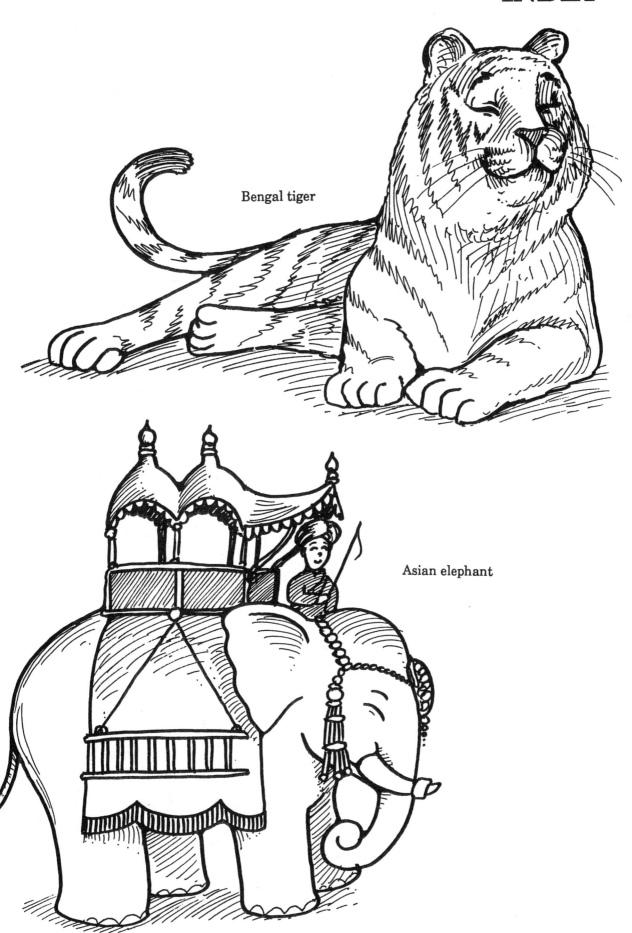

Bengal tiger

Asian elephant

The Taj Mahal

A boy learns to play the sitar.

snake charmer

Indian dancer

ISRAEL

Ostriches are a
common sight in
Israel.

Palm trees in
southern Israel.

ISRAEL

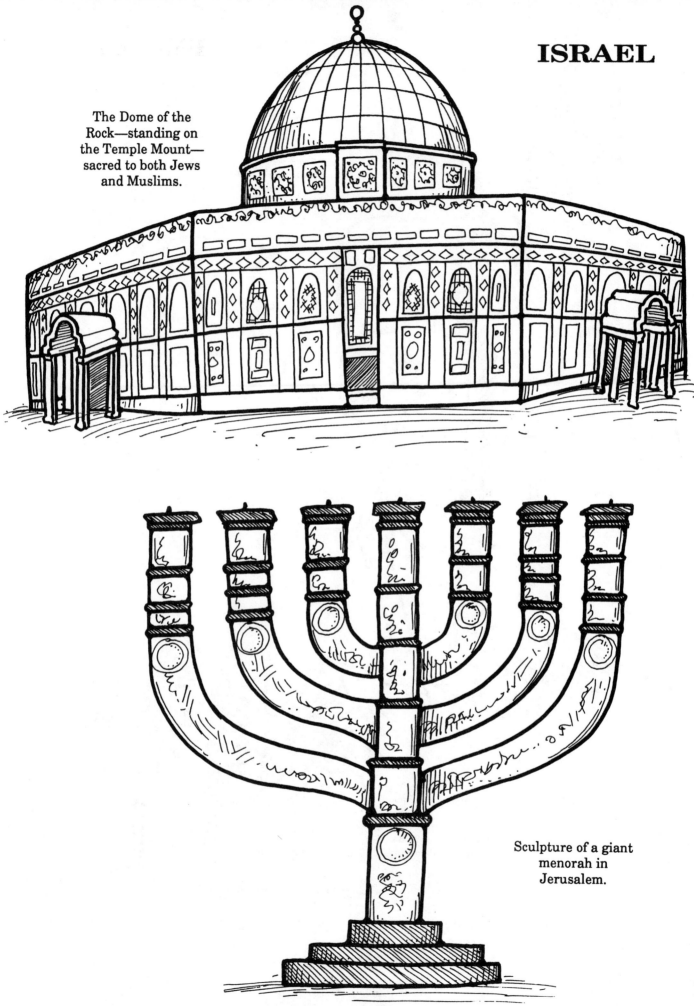

The Dome of the Rock—standing on the Temple Mount—sacred to both Jews and Muslims.

Sculpture of a giant menorah in Jerusalem.

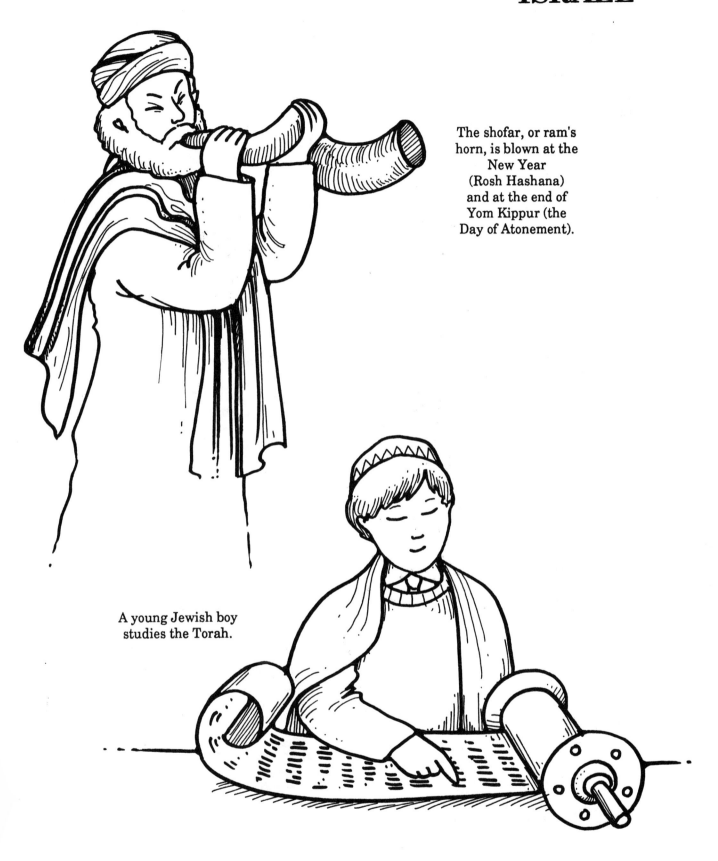

The shofar, or ram's horn, is blown at the New Year (Rosh Hashana) and at the end of Yom Kippur (the Day of Atonement).

A young Jewish boy studies the Torah.

ITALY

Spaghetti and
meatballs!

ancient
Roman chariot

Santa Maria del Fiore, Florence

ancient Roman colosseum

Leaning Tower of Pisa

opera singer

gondolier

JAPAN

cherry blossom

crane

bonsai tree

JAPAN

Mt. Fuji

Wood-block print by
Hokusai.

Statue of Buddha
at Kamakura.

NETHERLANDS

Porters carry a heavy load of golden Edam cheese to market at Alkmaar.

A Dutch boy holds an armful of tulips.

NETHERLANDS

Windmills once
powered the pumps
which kept the land
drained of water.

On December 6, the Dutch celebrate the birthday of St. Nicholas. The patron saint of children, he arrives by barge to hand out presents.

RUSSIA

RUSSIA

arctic lemming

117-year-old man

reindeer

RUSSIA

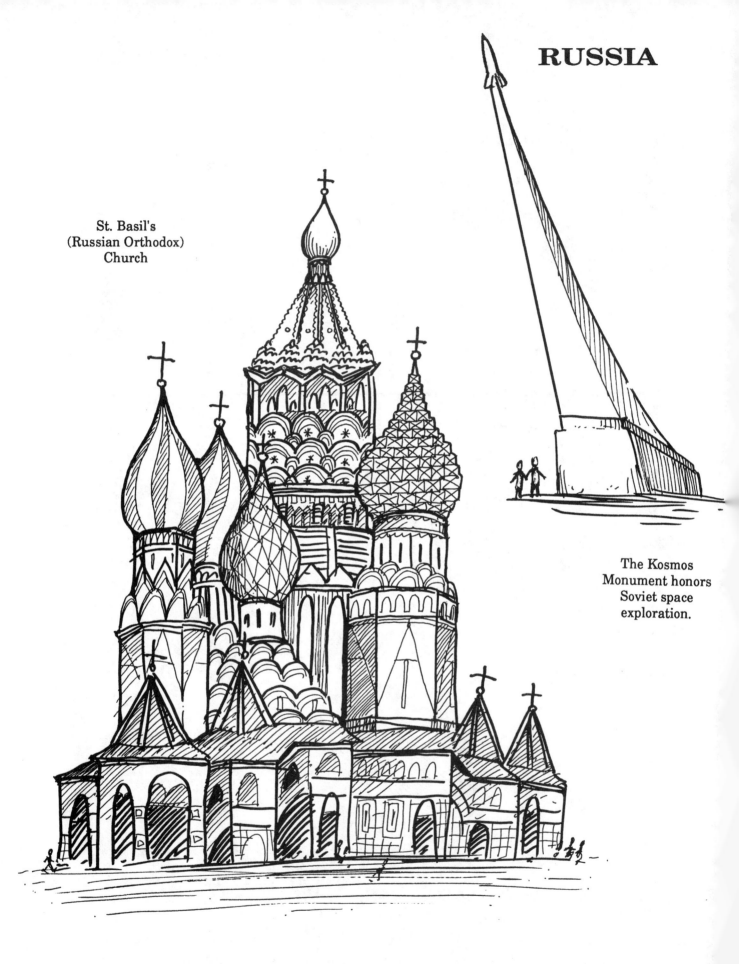

St. Basil's
(Russian Orthodox)
Church

The Kosmos
Monument honors
Soviet space
exploration.

RUSSIA

Russian circus

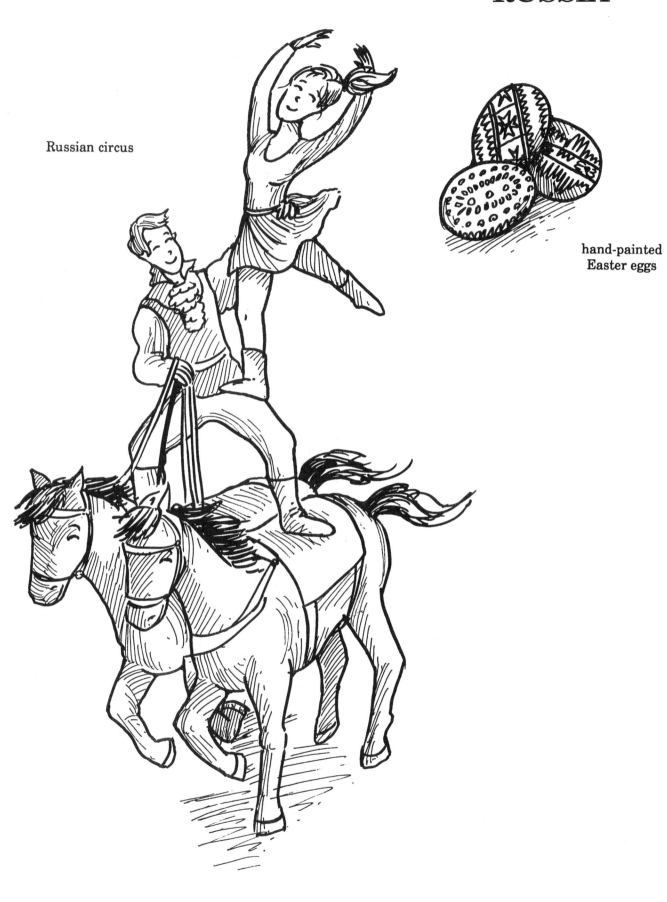

hand-painted
Easter eggs

Schoolchildren learn
to play the violin.

wooden
Matrioska dolls

Ballet pupils stage a
show in Moscow.

SPAIN

SPAIN

Man
harvesting olives.

donkey cart

SPAIN

fourteenth-century
castle in Castile

cathedral in Old
Barcelona

windmills in Toledo

flamenco dancer

Children in a circle dance.

bull-fighting

SWEDEN

SWEDEN

bilberries

Swedish brown bear

A woman dressed in old-fashioned clothes takes her goat out for a walk.

ancient
Viking ship

SWEDEN

Accompanied by her attendants, a young girl is dressed as St. Lucia with a crown of candles for December 13— Saint Lucia Day.

Men and boys in Lapland still wear brightly colored tunics and the cap of the Four Winds.

Midsummer Eve brings much celebration and dancing around the May pole.

THAILAND

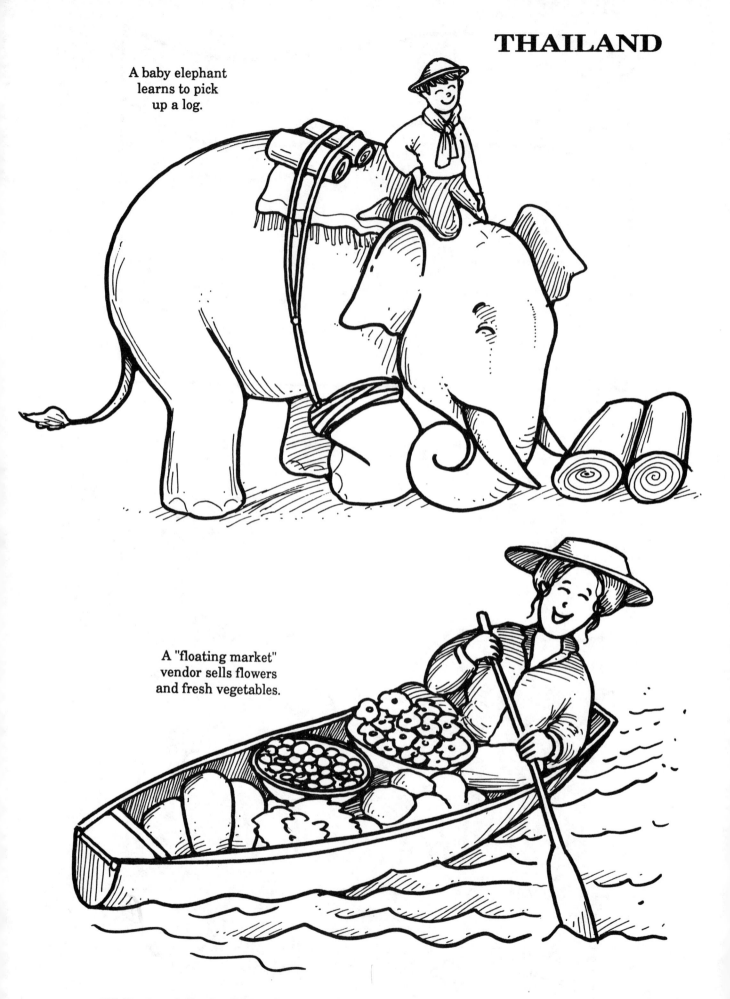

A baby elephant
learns to pick
up a log.

A "floating market"
vendor sells flowers
and fresh vegetables.

THAILAND

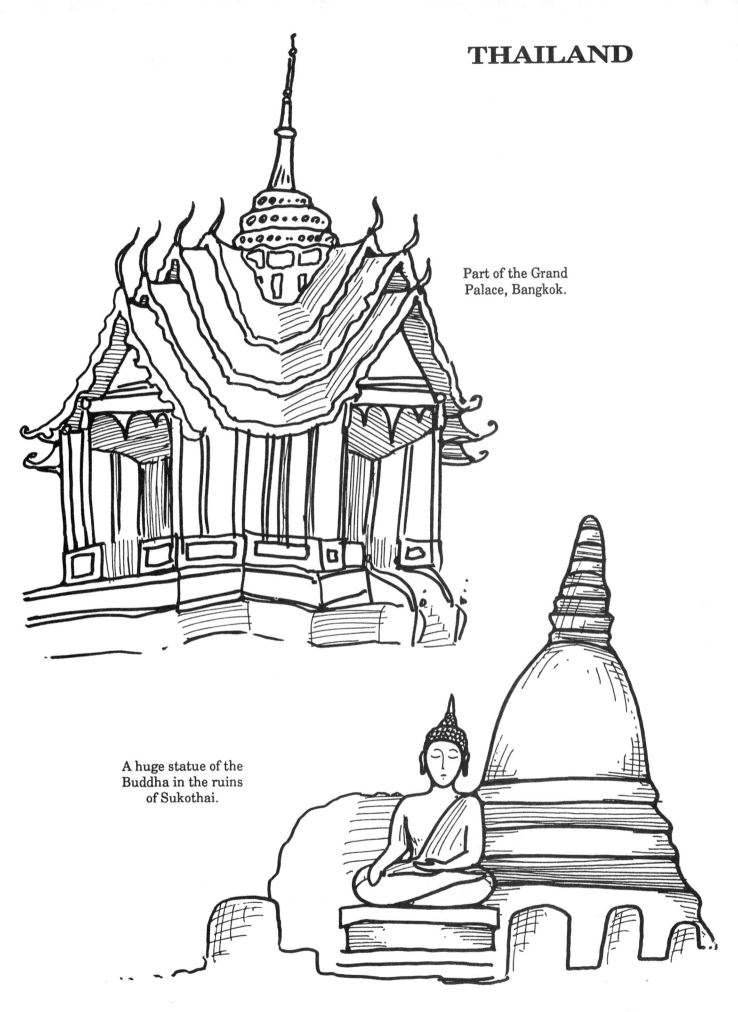

Part of the Grand
Palace, Bangkok.

A huge statue of the
Buddha in the ruins
of Sukothai.

Buddhist monks

Girl painting designs
on a paper and
bamboo umbrella.

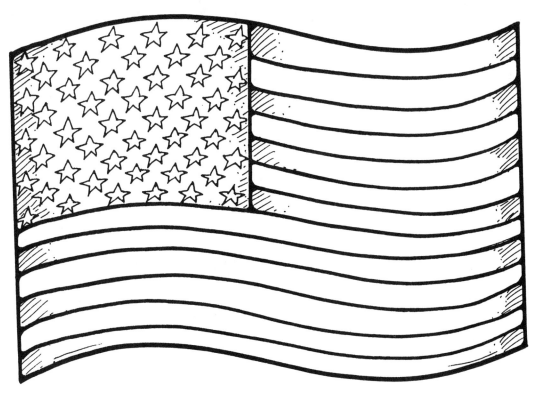

UNITED STATES

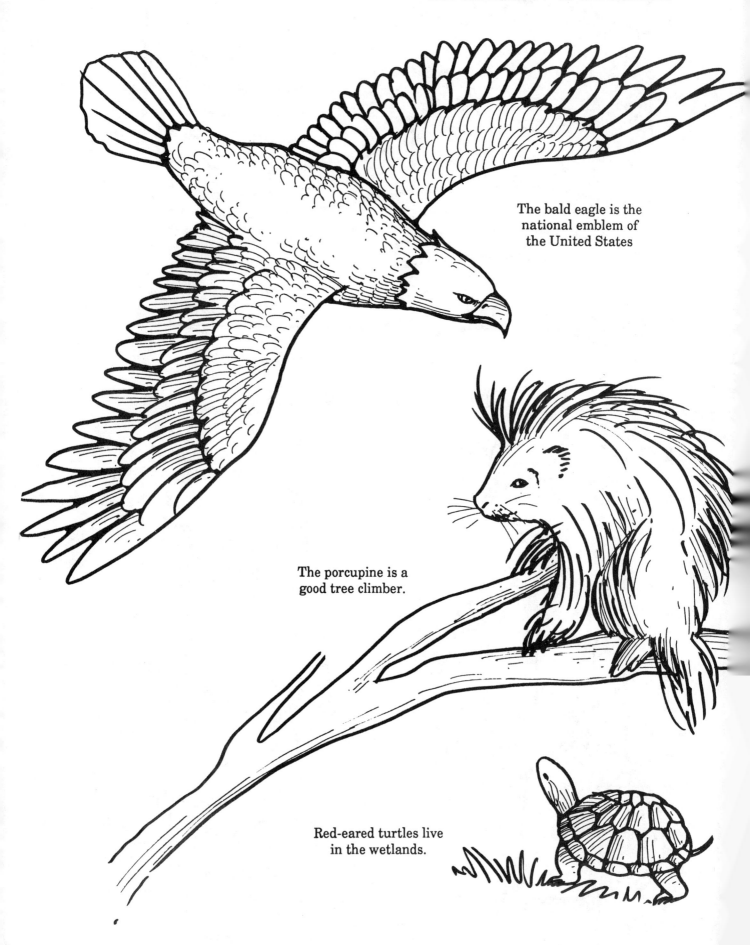

The bald eagle is the national emblem of the United States

The porcupine is a good tree climber.

Red-eared turtles live in the wetlands.

UNITED STATES

The United States
Capitol in
Washington, D.C.

The Golden Gate
Bridge spans across
San Francisco Bay
in California.

The Statue of Liberty
in New York Harbor
reminds people of
the millions who
came to America from
other lands in search
of freedom.

A Navaho woman weaves cloth on a loom.

Baseball is the national sport of the United States.

space shuttle

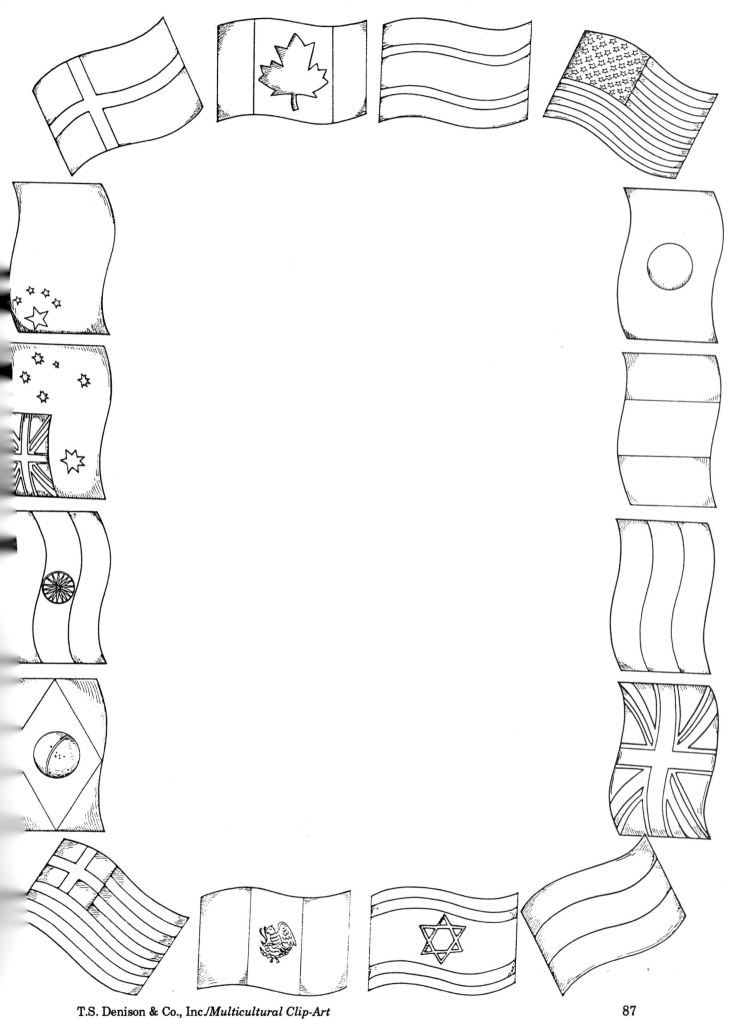

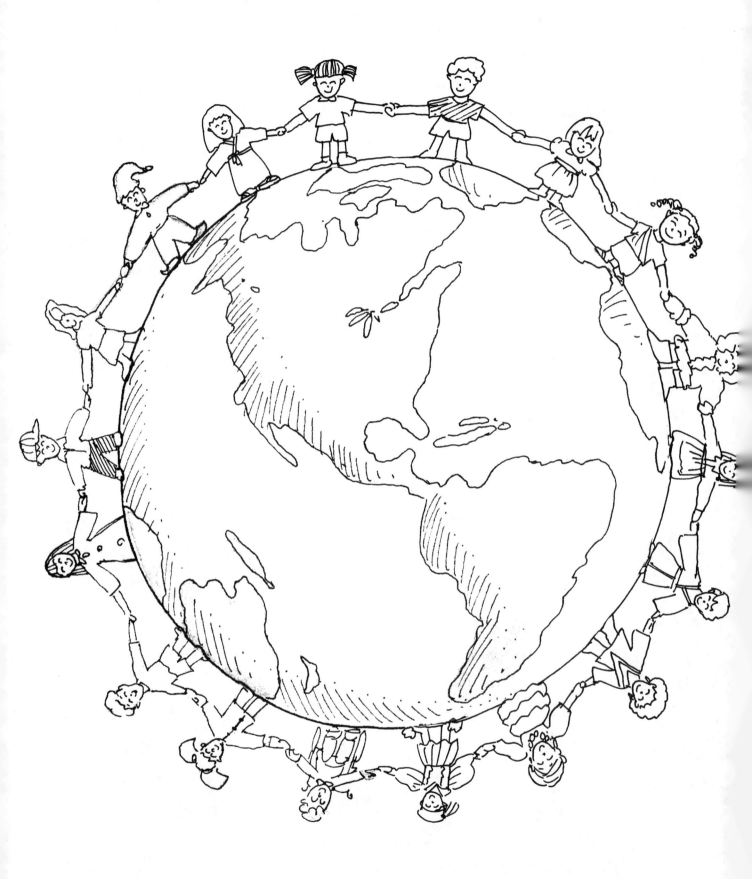

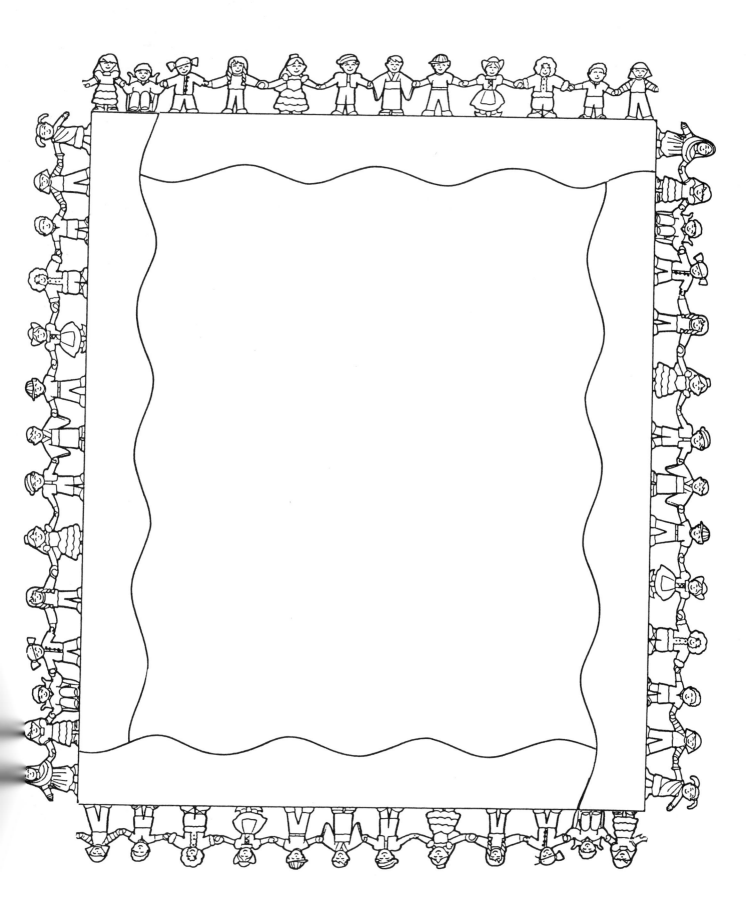